# THE SECOND SEASON

## LENT EASTER ASCENSION

**Wayne Saffen**

Fortress Press    Philadelphia

To the congregations of
St. Gregory of Nyssa Lutheran Church
at the University of Chicago 1960-72

*Library of Congress Catalog Card Number 72–87064*
*ISBN 0–8006–0144–0*

3463 H72   Printed in the United States of America   1-144

# CONTENTS

THE Second Season of the Church Year revolves around Easter. It is the heart of the *kerygma*: the basic announcement of what God has done for man in Jesus Christ. It focuses on the suffering, death, burial, descent, resurrection, and ascension of the God-man, Jesus Christ.

This is the basic "myth" out of which we live as Christians. It is the story we have to tell. It is the drama with which we identify in our own lives. We go with Christ to the cross. We die with him and rise again in baptism. We experience resurrection as God's life triumphs over our death. We sense the mystery of what God will make of us in Christ.

"Our humanity sits with God in Christ in heaven," says Martin Luther. "He became what we are that we might become what he is," said early church fathers. "We are changed into his likeness from glory to glory," said Saint Paul.

Jesus is *theanthropos*, the Godman. Christmas is the mystery of the incarnation of God in man. Resurrection is God's victory of life over death. Ascension deals with the future of man. The deification of man by the Spirit is set against the reification of man by technocracy. In the church God is transforming the body of humanity into the body of Christ. In Jesus, God is humanized and man is deified into one new Being with two natures, divine-human, each participating in the qualities of the other.

That basic drama of the redemption and transformation of man in Jesus Christ is what *The Second Season* is about.

# LENT

# LENT

Lent is
Forty days till Easter,
Not counting Sundays.

Lent is actually
Six and a half weeks
Of very violet repentance
And very purple passion.

Lent is
Watching a man go to his death
And not being able to stop it.

Lent is
Helping send him
To the cross.

Lent is
Knowing this
And letting it sink in.

Lent is
Not getting off
The hook.

Lent is
Taking sin seriously,
Taking life seriously,
Taking death seriously,
Taking everything
More seriously
Than usual.

Lent is,
Among other things,
Having to wait for Spring.

Lent is
Six more weeks
Of shivering
In the cold.

Lent is
Not a very happy time.
But it is what
You have to go through
To get to Easter.

Text I: *Psalm 102:9–10*

For I eat ashes like bread,

  and mingle tears with my drink,

because of thy indignation and anger;

  for thou hast taken me up and thrown me away.

Text II: Ezekiel 28

Text III: "Deformities & Hemorrhaging Laid to Forest Spray."

*New York Times,* February 8, 1970, p. 60.

# THE ASHES OF MODERNITY

SO here we are again, beginning Lent again, talking about ashes again, being quaintly liturgical and irrelevant to modern men (so they say), "doing our thing," which doesn't seem to have anything to do with anything, quoting Bible like it meant something and hanging crepe like somebody's dead or dying, being lugubrious, morose, pessimistic, alarmist, and generally cantankerous about the human condition.

And so, somehow, for whatever reasons, groups of people gather themselves in churches quite used to deadly pollution in cities and in towns and hamlets underneath spreading smog to talk about whatever it is you talk about on Ash Wednesday. In quainter times we would mark foreheads with ashes from last year's Palm Sunday palms and say to each of you: "Remember, O man, that you are dust, and to dust you shall return." This being the post-Christian era of the Secular City, industry swabs our lungs with carcinogenic materials and Detroit's purple people eaters spew all over the city, turning the blue sky grey. So we trade the ashes of liturgy, which denoted repentance, for the ashes of modernity, which are laden with death. This is the price of Progress. "What's good for production is good for the country." "Better things for better living through chemistry." "When residents eat smoke, it means people are working." Are you a miner with black lung? Tell it to Congress. Are you an urban respiratory case? Tell it to City Council. Had enough?

What shall we talk about this Ash Wednesday? Palm leaf ashes? Crosses on foreheads? Sin? Pollution? Pollution it must be. It is the "in" topic. Pollution is the ash of modernity which assaults human life. It brings the country together again. It gives a political platform for candidates, incumbents, and challengers alike. It promises to be a financial bonanza, as the industries which polluted our atmosphere will now get contracts to clean it up. Is this repentance?

If we hear that the ashes of modernity is pollution, already we are tuned in. Ash Wednesday is "relevant" again. Glory be, liturgy saved by industry! And, immediately, as you all tune in, you all tune out. Do you really want the preacher to fulminate against pollution? Shall we count the ways? Shall we heap up horror stories to make you properly angry? Shall we turn you out of church this evening charged up like raging beasts to "do something" about pollution, ready to fall upon smokestacks and topple them to the ground? Shall we send you forth to pinch shut automobile exhaust pipes or join organizations which buy up stocks in companies to confront stockholders in their meetings or withhold electric bill payments? Shall we name the dragons, so you may go out and slay them?

We shall not do that. We shall preach the word of God, which calls for repentance as the plain message of Lent. Dust will do for symbol, quite a literal symbol in every respect, especially for pollutants. The word of God has the characteristic of a word spoken to the human condition which requires that we heed it to live. The price of ignoring it is death. The word of God in this instance is quite clear: either we stop polluting and poisoning our environment and take remedial steps immediately or we shall die poisoned by our own effluence of affluence. The word of God is the word Reality speaks to our human condition. The word of God is not simply something which speaks to those who are religiously inclined. You cannot take it or leave it. You heed it, or else!

The word of God about pollutants has not been proclaimed by preachers, at least not initially. It has been preached by scientists, ecologists, reformers. It did not reach the president through the voice of court preachers in King's Chapel at the White House but by reports from the scientific community. It reached other politicos when it looked like a viable political issue. It reached the stage of public consciousness because pollution is universal sin and the wages of sin is death. It is as simple as that.

If it be sin, it is beyond politics, although politics will be part of its solution. Sin requires repentance and a whole new way of life. This is true of individuals and society. The Ash Wednesday message today is the standard cartoon lampooning the bearded prophet: "Repent or die." We always laughed at that one. We aren't laughing any more. We are too busy coughing from eating dust.

There is something deeply wrong with human nature that we have come into such great peril. There are some theological indictments to be made. The industrial revolution and its resultant pollution rest upon the idea of man's dominance over nature in such a way that we imagined men were not part of nature. The heresy involved is docetic. To deny our grounding to earth, to imagine we can live cerebrally alone, to imagine if we just build our apartments high enough in our modern Babels we can escape the earth by living in the sky, to think we do not make a human trade, an exchange, every time we create an artificial environment, is illusory, demonic, sin.

The day we exchanged the word of God for the deification of scientific, technical reason, to conquer the earth and rape and exploit it for the mere comfort and convenience of some people—that day we began a new idolatrous religion and created a new future for illusion. Religion is no longer the prevailing illusion. Technology is. Until we return science and technical reason to the control of a good human will for the sake of human beings, we shall continue to create the kingdom of death, sacrificing real live human beings to real dead technology. No Moloch of ancient times was the devourer of human beings that our military-industrial complex is. Idolatry is sin. The wages of sin is death. That is the word of God. We may wrestle with it all we want, and deny it. We shall not prevail against the word of

God. We shall die trying. So, let us eat dust and learn repentance.

Theology, instead of serving human beings, creations of the loving God, has served the idol Moloch. We rejoiced over the disenthrallment of nature. We gave theological warrant for laying sinful human hands on nature to tear it apart and yield its secrets. We said this was man's vocation, when God in Genesis made man lord of the earth to subdue it. We learned to treat nature as a thing rather than that mysterious organism in which we live and move and have our being. And nature yielded, doing what it does. It has tried patiently to teach us about the conditions of our human existence. Irrigation brought salt to some Western valleys, driving farmers out. We created a dustbowl in the Midwest, from which we have only recently recovered. We stripped the trees and bushes from California hillsides to plant houses, and wondered why they were washed down by mudslides.

The final irony is that we shall never destroy the earth, although we have murdered all forms of life in insatiable lust and greed. If animals could vote, they might be glad to see us exterminate ourselves and leave them in peace. Nature will survive us. But we shall never survive nature when we destroy her life-giving properties for insane ends. Nature is not in trouble. She can heal herself. We are in trouble, until we admit to creatureliness again. That is the word of God to us. Deny it, if we will. We shall never win that argument.

The profit motive easily becomes greed, one of the seven deadly sins. It makes a virtue out of covetousness, which the Ten Commandments condemn. In the name of profit motive every sin against man and nature has been justified in the capitalist world. A system built upon justified greed is organized sin. We shall have to get used to that judgment. It may be biblically orthodox, but it is heretical as a contradiction to the very basis of the American economic creed.

Karl Marx was right when he said that the land belongs to the people and that capital exploited the two givens, land and labor, for the sake of private gain and privilege. The Psalmist agrees with him: "The earth is the Lord's and the fullness thereof." According to quite orthodox Christian doctrine, nothing belongs to anybody. All that we own as we occupy it for a while is a stewardship held in trust for mankind. If we violate that trust and exploit land or people for our own gain, we are quite simply sinners biblically and criminals politically.

Pollution is a crime against people, a crime against nature, a crime against God. Exploitation is a crime against people, a crime against nature, a crime against God. Military suppression of conscience is a crime against people, a crime against nature, and a crime against God. If we think these are not sins which will be punished by the living God, we are ignorant of history and of God's word, which says just that. God has done it before, time and time again. He will do it again.

Freud spoke of religion as the future of illusion. But illusion has more futuristic options than religion. A secular world has to deal now with illusions of freedom and reason and the problem of human will. We are mystified: the problem of pollution is so self-evident, yet it is so hard to do anything about it. We are angry, yet feel helpless. We threaten and cajole, organize and lobby. Yet pollution is surely a human product, created by human decisions, about which something can be done. We are not wrestling with some blind fate, over which we have no power, as we might if we suffered from earthquake or tornado or tidal wave. A manufacturing process and system devised by human beings can be changed by human beings. Then why is it so hard to do so? If to see is to be able to do, why can we not do what we see obviously needs doing? If reason is master of things earthly, how is it that reason serves such irrational processes, against our own self-interest? We know in advance that the "war against pollution" will be a financial boondoggle which will make many rich and leave the nation polluted. Do we doubt this? What happened to our "War on Poverty"? That was an easy war to win. Why have we not won it? "War against Racism" is also an easy war to win. Why have we not won it?

The problem lies in the human will. Let us admit with Martin Luther that the will is not free but bound in sin. We cannot but sin. "The good we would do we fail to do; the evil we do not want to do, that is what we do." When Saint Paul sees these contradictory wills at work within himself, he perceives it as working death. "Who shall deliver us from the body of this death?" he asks. Who, indeed?

All our energies drive us to death and destruction unless our will is liberated and redirected toward life. That is a hard word. It offends our sense of free will. Then let us go with your free will and wipe the skies clean of death, cleanse the rivers, make the manufacturers shape up or close down. We know we cannot do that. We are overwhelmed with helplessness and anger and rage. We experience impotence.

We are not free. We only imagine that we are. This is not a free country. We only say we are. Although the solution is within the president's power to insist upon by requesting legislation enabling him to act, we know he won't, that he is not free to do what needs to be done. Although Congress could pass laws, we know that its members are beholden to special interests. At every turn we discover that there is some specious reason which prevents us from being able to do what obviously could be done, if only the will were free to do what is right. So let's admit it. We are dominated by a sinful will, and it's killing us.

Then perhaps we could have a real Ash Wednesday, as the seriousness of our plight descends upon us. There must be a reformation of head and members of society. The powers-that-be must change or be destroyed, even as they destroy us all. That is a word of God which is spoken first in words, giving man a chance to repent. If he does not repent, the spoken word will be done.

The word of God will do what it says. If we will not hear the word which is spoken we shall have to deal with the word as it is done. God does what he says. He shall surely destroy our nation by war or revolution if we do not repent, or let us strangle in our impotent power. It is the latter which will more likely happen. We shall prepare ourselves for wars which will never come, unless we lash out in fear to prevent them in distant places and call down wrath upon ourselves at home. We will multiply warhead installations and plant the seeds of death all over the world. One day they will all begin to leak: nerve gas, nuclear poisons, the death which will not stay buried coming back to haunt us as ghosts from Ash Wednesdays past.

We have made the national decision that we are quite willing to wipe out all human life on our planet to secure our position of pre-eminence as a world power. That is what we call our "national interest." Thereby we make ourselves the enemies of mankind, and our own chief enemy as well. Already we are killing off our own people with an evil as banal as pollution. What will be the judgment of God upon us if we do not repent? Do we need to draw pictures? What else can we do, if we desire salvation, than to repent? What would lead us to repent? Only the clear word of God that it is our only alternative to death, that unless we repent we perish. What if we hear the word and will not heed it? Then we shall surely die.

This is an awesome Ash Wednesday. Our text is not simply words from the Bible relevant to our condition or words from the Sunday paper which describe it, but the very poisoned air we breathe every day of our lives in this place. Something should be getting to us Americans pretty soon. It is hard to have a more real word than one we choke on and which coats our lungs with death.

We start Lent again every Ash Wednesday. We follow the way of the cross again. That way leads into conflicts with every established interest in society, church, and state in Jesus' world. This conflict has everything to do with salvation. The cost of salvation comes high. It costs innocent suffering and death to deliver man from his sin, to set him on the way to life instead of on the way to death. It took the life of God's own Son to redeem the world from sin. That is the only human sacrifice necessary and adequate to atone for the world's sin and redeem us all. Jesus Christ on the cross is God's own sacrifice complete for all people everywhere. No more human sacrifice is needed ever again. Yet human sacrifice is still the price of human progress. God does not want anything but living sacrifices, people who come from death to life to live in his kingdom. It is the consumer gods on earth who eat people, who must be appeased by human sacrifices before they will yield concessions. Human sacrifice is the price we have to pay when we confront entrenched corporate special interests which devour people for profit. When we bring the word of God's judgment to these idols and their idolaters, we must pay the price. We shall put the finger on sin and not let up the pressure. Let every abscess throb with pain till lanced.

Let's get it straight. We are not imploring the consumer gods to lower their levels of pollution. We do not pray to them as humble suppliants, appealing to their good will, when it is only the profit motive and self-interest they acknowledge. We shall not be like half a million people praying to the president in Washington for peace while he watched a football game on television. We do not pray to them, for they are not gods. They have no power that God did not give them or that he can't take away. We speak in the name of God for the people that they shall repent or die, their kingdoms smashed. We are armed with the word of God and the power of God. They need not heed the prayers of the people. They cannot possibly avoid the judgment of the word of God.

On this Ash Wednesday God is serving an eviction notice on this society which fouls the earth. When we go outside, we can already smell the sulphur, the fire and brimstone.

Repent or eat ashes and perish. This is the word of God to us on Ash Wednesday. It does not encourage or flatter us. But it still gives us time. It does offer life and salvation. There are alternatives. We could grasp life instead of death. But we can hardly say that God's word to us today lacks definition in terms we can understand. When we eat dust for bread, we begin to get the point.

---

* This sermon was preached in Augustana Lutheran Church of Hyde Park at the University of Chicago as the decade of the 1970s began. The air outside was unusually polluted in the highest pollution area of Chicago. The preacher was in the middle of a month-long bout with a severe bronchial infection irritated by the pollution, and could scarcely speak. The unintended effect was overwhelming. The sermon was rewritten for publication on the very day the Supreme Court ruled 4 to 3 that the nuclear test at Amchitka could go on, turning down requests of conservationists for an injunction against it. Dangers of ecological peril cited were overruled by the majority vote. So was the worldwide protest. The event confirmed the thesis of this sermon, in this writer's opinion. The balance of that historic decision lay in the mind of one man and how he thought, what "word" he listened to when he tried to reach a decision.

We have a tendency
To overrate temptation
And to underrate it.

W E tend to think of temptation in grandiose terms.
Actually, it confronts us in little things.
We like to think we would resist temptations
(Or yield to them) which are so marvelous
We will never get a chance to test ourselves against them.
Imagined temptations are wishful thinking.
We are quite safe from them, except in fantasy.
We do not take temptation seriously when it really comes
Because it seems so small, so obvious, or so concealed,
So unimportant that we don't recognize it for what it is.

Temptation is what we will sell out for.
It prices our integrity, values our soul, tests our character.
Every man has his price. What is embarrassing
Is how cheaply we sell out.
It is life that tests us, God who tries us.
It is the false lure that gets us every time.

We think of temptation in grandiose terms,
Of Faust, the Devil and Daniel Webster,
Big time gamblers, embezzlers, wine, women, and song,
The reach for power in empire or high finance,

Achieving the hero's fame and glory,
Coveting the admiration of millions, the devotion of minions.
Temptations overcome make heroes.
If the temptation be great enough,
Losers and scoundrels still make history.
Win or lose, we'd like to take our chance at the big one.

Jesus' temptation comes at the outset of his career.
Successfully resisted, it will not go away.
It will accompany him at each point of decision.
The first hurdle of temptation is to test resolve
At the beginning, when ideals are high.
Temptation permits us to choose our own goals,
And then promises to help us get what we want, at a price.
The first temptation is important. It clarifies our goals.
The last temptation can come in a garden of prayer or on a cross.
It is the anguish that we may have chosen wrong.

Jesus fasted forty days in the wilderness.
Self-discipline, self-denial, self-knowledge
Are important to really think things out,
To ready oneself for ordeal, set oneself toward life.
Appetites must be brought under subjection
So they do not dominate, deter, and dictate to us.
Otherwise there is no temptation at all,
Only the search for satisfaction.

The first temptation is gratification of the senses.
Food now, bread now, meat now, liquor now, sex now.
If we will sell out for immediate sensual satisfaction,
There is very little that won't tempt us.
We are easy marks.
Deprivation sharpens appetites.
Renunciation means something.
Everyone knows this temptation is real enough
Who has tried to stop smoking, stop drinking, go on a diet.
The reward of bread at the end of a fast sounds reasonable.
If one can command stones to become bread, why not?

Jesus answers that man does not live by bread alone
But by every word that proceeds from the mouth of God.
But man doesn't live by words alone, either.
Hunger is real, and words won't fill it.
Spirit is real, too;
Neither bread nor liquor will satisfy it.
Men eat to live. We live and die by words.
The spirit that keeps us alive thrives on words.

The second temptation is instant fame.
One feat catapults the hero into the public eye.
Lindbergh flies the Atlantic alone.
Columbus discovers America.
Magellan voyages around the world.

Astronauts walk on the moon.
Men go over Niagara Falls in a barrel
Or walk across it on a tightrope.
Movie stars have press agents,
Celebrity their substitute for fame.
Notoriety will do for some who crave publicity.
"I don't care what they say about me,
So long as they spell my name right,"
Is the new measure of celebrity status.
Fame is hard won; it rests on achievement.
Jonas Salk conquers polio,
Surgeons transplant hearts,
Albert Einstein's equations come out right.
Jesus can take the short cut of spectacle to achieve fame
Or take the long route of preaching and healing
To develop a following.
Einstein once advised a young man:
"Become a value, not a success."
Jesus says to Satan: "We should not tempt God."
God may protect fools, drunkards, and children.
Daredevils take their own risks.

The third temptation
Is to stand on a hill overlooking Los Angeles or San Francisco
Imagining one can own it all.

It is not an impossible dream,
When one man practically owned Nevada, another Greece,
Another Saudi Arabia, another Iran.
To be president of the United States
Is to be the most powerful man in the world.
The pinnacle of power is heady.
Unlimited wealth is a real lure.
It is not that it can't be gained,
Although it never really can be held.
It is what it costs that impedes better men.
Those who seek to accumulate wealth can succeed.
But to succeed in such business
Makes wealth the goal of life,
Material possessions the proof of success and human worth.
One need only give up his humanity, his soul, his spirit, his joy,
To become the owner and possessor of everything but himself.
When we worship goods, we make gods
Out of the systems which secure and protect them.
Jesus resists. "We should worship God and serve him only."
God is the only owner of all we say we own,
Good and gracious Giver of every good and perfect gift.

Temptations are most real when we are persuaded
That giving in to them will achieve our noblest purposes.
Everybody yields, usually settling for less,

And being disappointed in the bargain.
A man to watch would be the one who resists.
He gains the enmity of all who yield.

The last temptation is the acid test.
Is it really worth giving up everything to end on a cross?
Jesus' answer is that he did not come to get; he came to give.
He gave his life for all men's life everywhere.
He had no possessions; so he was free.
The state would provide a cross.
We always have public money for death.
The instrument would do for the purpose.
The gift Christ gives for everyone is life's salvation.
No one gives up his soul to get it; he gets his soul back intact.
Salvation is free. It can't be bought or bargained for.
To believe this is to have a set of values
Which inoculate against the virus of coveting.

Temptations are important.
They force us to admit what we really want out of life.
They can be resisted; but only if we mean it.

It is because we do yield to temptation
That we need forgiveness and a second chance.
What we need is help in fortifying the spirit.
What we need is God alive and well in us.

RELIGIOUS exclusiveness and intolerance breed religious wars.
Insoluble conflicts fester through centuries
To break out in new epidemics of old hatreds.
Protestants and Catholics, Jews and Arabs, Christians and communists,
Conflicting absolutes send men to the killing ground.

Religious peculiarity gives a sense of identity.
Group consciousness solidifies a like-minded people.
National religion mobilizes against outsiders as inferior.
As if the only valid human history were one's own.
The stranger has always been the enemy; so says anthropology.
Insiders define outsiders to keep them out; so says sociology.
Jesus, of all people, sounds like an insider
Putting down an outsider, a woman come to him for help.
Was Jesus a male chauvinist, an ethnic snob, a religious bigot?

The situation was basically human.
It called for no other definition.
A woman's daughter was bedevilled, disturbed, in mental pain.
What parent would not be distraught trying to deal with that?
Jesus helped people. Everybody knew that.
What situation could have been simpler?

There was, however minor, a problem to be dealt with.
They did belong to conflicting nationalities, religions.
National and religious prejudices intrude.
They must be dealt with.

# CHILDREN'S BREAD FOR DOGS?

**LENT II**
Matthew 15:21–28

20

Centuries of war have embittered Israeli and Syrian neighbors.
Golan Heights overlooking Galilean villages
Have more than once blooded the Sea of Galilee.
National prejudices ought not be; but there they are.
War distorts, destroys basic human relationships,
Alienating neighbors, making enemies across boundary lines.
Even in peace, we are conscious of our nationality
When we cross borders into another's territory.

We know that people respond out of their prejudices.
We do not expect Jesus to be a superiority snob of the ethnic stripe.
The Syrian woman called him "Son of David."
It was a compliment of recognition he could hardly ignore.
He needn't have given the Jewish sign of exclusiveness.
He was in her country; she wasn't in his.
He didn't have to sound like a noisy American
Bragging his way through Europe.
Unresponsive, arrogant, he simply ignored her.

Following after, she kept crying out,
Creating a bothersome, embarrassing, public scene.
Disciples did what disciples always do.
Insiders always act that way.
They asked Jesus to send her away.
It might have been kinder if he did.

His response was an unconscionable slur:
"I am not sent except for the lost sheep of the house of Israel."
What doctor, with his Hippocratic oath,
Would be so insensitive to plain human need?
What kind of man would say a cruel and vicious thing
To a woman in trouble, humiliating her in public?
Would the "lost sheep" of the house of Israel
Find his arrogant exclusiveness any more charming?


She fell at his knees, begging, "Help *me*!"
The issue was not Syrians versus Israelis.
It was a simple human problem.
A woman, a human being, needed help.
Do not see a Syrian, Doctor.
Do not see a human being as simply black or yellow or white.
See a woman in need. Help *her*!


Jesus did not help her.
In later centuries Christians could sing, believing,
"Help of the helpless, O abide with me."
Jesus was of no help to this helpless person.
"It is not right to take the children's bread
and give it to the dogs."
That was his answer.

No human being has to take that kind of talk from another.
Pride should muster itself and leave such a man forthwith.
How can there be healing or humanity, let alone salvation,
Coming from racist, religiously exclusive, ethnic bigotry?
Was Jesus just a quoter of bad folk proverbs which do not fit?

We might expect a demagogue, some loud-mouthed politician,
Knowing his constituency where his vote depends,
To talk like that. But a savior? Never!
Such a man can rouse the rabble and incite riots.
He can fan religious hysteria and become a populist hero,
Exploiting people's hatred as his political base.
The milk of human kindness is what saviors need to nurse on.
If this insolence were all that Jesus had to offer,
There never would have been a New Testament or Christian faith.
Jesus would not have been worth remembering or following.

The woman did not go home, even after this final cruel insult.
What comparison could have been more odious?
Jews are the children of God? Syrians are dogs?
Then go home and feed your children, Jew, and learn how dogs
    can bite.
That's what we would have answered, every one of us.
Not this woman! She went with him measure for measure.
"What you say is true, Lord. It is also true
That dogs may eat crumbs which fall from the master's table."

She wasn't asking to be accepted as a Jew.
What she was asking was important to her, not to him.
To him it was just crumbs thrown to a dog.
His argument argued for her, not against her.

Would a man kick a dog, or a woman, who is down, grovelling?
Of course not. Nor was this his intent.
"Woman, your faith is very great.
It will be done for you as you will."

Happy ending?
What are we to make of an encounter like that?
Jesus seems to be completely out of character.
We are used to him telling off religious snobs, not being one.
We are used to him defending outcasts, not adding to persecution.
It was he, after all, who made a hero out of a good Samaritan.

Beneath the calculated insult and its riposte,
Beneath the prejudicial rhetoric
A real divine-human encounter took place.

Do we find his behavior shocking?
If we do, dare we claim to find it strange,
As if people did not deal with each other this way,
Vaunting their superiority over others by treating them as inferiors?
Do we not pull out all the stops of racial pride and prejudice
To swell the organ sound of our own religious supremacy?

Do we not wince to hear these words in Jesus' mouth?
Do not these words and proverbs haunt us with familiarity?
Have we not used them often to describe some other group?
Have we not through all our Christian centuries
Closed off from our communions other folks not quite like us?
"Feed not that which is holy to dogs,
Neither cast your pearls before swine."
These words of Jesus have justified untold cruelties.

Jesus breaks the categories of categorical thinking.
It is not Syrian and Jew who confront each other in this moment.
It is a man and a woman, a patient and a doctor.
None of the religious or national or ethnic categories
Constructed out of human imagination and pride
Can hold in the face of two actual human beings.

Jesus transcends all arbitrary, separating distances,
To create a new humanity out of all conflicting groups.
Faith knows this, and refuses to go with categories.

There is henceforth no more Jew or Greek,
Slave or free, male or female—for all are one in Christ,
Transcending all arbitrary differences.
Jesus and the woman alone knew what was going on.
The rest of us are just finding out.

# ON CASTING OUT DEVILS

ALL kinds of demons possess people.
    We have not named the devils, only their victims:
Schizophrenic, paranoid, megalomanic, trapezoid,
Manic-depressive, depravoid, confusional states multiployed.
What primitive had more awesome ghosts and goblins to haunt him?
Sophistication merely covers ignorance.
Words have no meaning until they are known.

Mumbo jumbo, cant and credo, hallucinate, relieve the tense, so
Hocus-pocus, make the mostest, devils bore and bores bedevil,
Beelzebub has hiccups and Satan's turned to satin,
The devils all have fled into the center of the head
Where mesmerized and memorized they plagiarize the dead.
Nonexistents conjured out of craniums calmly blow their smoke rings
Through huff-a-puffy nostrils that dilate in disdain.
They go, they disappear, they leave, they split, depart.

When Jesus casts out devils, he throws them out of people.
They do not leave willingly. They protest grotesquely. But they go.
Always, from Christ to Freud, this raises arguments.
How does he do it?

The victim was dumb, uncommunicative, detached, sunken into
    silence.
A wall of silence keeping safe from everyone without
Protects outside others from the hell within.
Spectators look and wonder why such silence shuts them out.
In fear of infection, our malice parades as righteousness
To isolate, ridicule, label, burn, destroy, annihilate
Those who are disturbed by all the free-floating anxieties
That devils ride on. Like miasmic clouds of monster gas,
They enter mind by eye and ear to hold their slaves in mental thrall.
The disturbed are disturbers of our peace.
We will not be at peace until we know what disturbs them.
Finding that, we are as likely to punish them for telling us as not.
Silence is a weapon of defense perfected by a sanity,
However mad, that acts instinctively to protect.

Who has power to break the silence?
Who can command the devils to come out?
At imperious commands the victim's fears contract
To keep the devils in. Devils do not yield to mere command.
The power of love and trust must first be loosed.
Victims must be able to afford to let go,
To let emotional cramps relax that tighten vocal cords in fear.
The devil cannot be expelled until the victim knows he's loved,
That he has nothing to fear from us, nor we from him.

How would the bedevilled know that, when we ourselves
Are source and reinforcement of some most vital fears?

Only he can throw the devils out who can be trusted
To love and heal the victim.

The command which banishes insubstantial fears
Does not come from power only, or from knowledge, but from love.
Having no substantial or plausible fears to justify the silence
Of self-protection, victims can relax and warm to human love again.
Jesus will not harm us or probe too deeply
To unearth secrets for uncertain reasons.
Warmth and trust communicate.
Only concern which is itself not anxious can relax the bedevilled.
If we would not add to misery but relieve it, we must start there.

Jesus does not fear those bedevilled nor their devils.
He knows the incommunicates, the strange, the strained.
Insane or raving lunatics do not drive him off.
Catatonics cannot shut him out.
Jesus knows what bedevils man is wholly insubstantial.
It can be thrown out by one who knows and loves.
When fear and terror relax their grip, the tense become relaxed.
Then, of course, the dumb can speak.
There is nothing amazing in this.
It happens all the time under therapeutic conditions.

People who judge behavior only often do not know
What to call underlying causes by any name other than devil.
It is our ignorance which gives insubstantial fears the name of devil,
And makes us fear both wraiths and their terribly tortured victims.
Devils feed on fears. When fears are gone,
There is nothing left for invisible persecutors to live on.

When Jesus spoke, the devils fled, and the dumb one spoke.
One would think whole crowds would rejoice upon seeing
A sick person untied from emotional knots, speaking freely.
But health from healing is often as baffling
As the sickness which precedes it.
As cause for sickness must be found (presumed)
So cause for healing must be found (presumed).
Everything must have a cause, we say, as if then we knew.
Facts must be accounted for. Otherwise, what shall we do with them?

Unseen powers must have intelligence, say prescientific minds.
Devils show a high degree of aptitude for dissimulation.
Things are not what they seem; but we always think they are.
Those who know least about what bedevils mankind
Are first to parade as experts on the invisible causes
Of war and economics and social injustice, of difficulties
Of personal maladjustment, all forms of public crisis.
It is, they say, a highly organized conspiracy of devils.
Some sort of hierarchy of demons is bent on chaos and confusion.

Little wonder, then, that some who saw said Jesus was demonic.
He was himself in league with Satan, said confident know-nothings.
Jesus casts out devils by Beelzebub, chief of devils. Imagine that:
The Lord of Glory in consort with the Lord of Flies!
Who else would know the devil's ways but a devil himself?
If the bedevilled are feared, healers are to be feared more
For understanding devils all too well.
It is a strange logic; but we know it well.
What other than an enlightened people could ascribe all human ills
To an international conspiracy of communists or capitalists?
We fear most that power which undermines the disorder we call order,
More comfortable with it than with the liberation of humanity
From all that imprisons, represses, dehumanizes us.
All our troubles come from outside sources, we protest.
The invisible enemy takes us unawares, stealing our confidences.
The devil comes into our midst always as some outside stranger.
We must persecute to protect what we call our sanity.

If Jesus could release religious fanatics from hysteria,
If Freud could probe the unmentionable thoughts which bedevil sex,
If Marx could call history economic and look with cool eye
And impassioned heart at all the structures of oppression
Which make men victims, daring them to arise and lose their chains,
If Darwin could demonstrate our link to the animal world,
No matter how we intellectualize our difference as superiority,
Then Reality has come upon us to threaten
All our constructs of ignorance we hold as dogma.

There is no escaping religious controversy
When Reality collides with illusion.
Illusion has no future as religion in the real world Jesus lives in.
God opens eyes to see what is there,
And opens ears to hear what is said in pain or silence.
If it is by the finger of God—that healing digit
Which touches the sure sore spot—that demons are expelled
From comfortable residence, then God's kingdom has come upon us.

The kingdom of God is the one thing we fear more than devils.
We prefer the occult to the rational, unaccountable causes
To accountable ones, false values to true ones, slavery
To freedom, fear to faith, social insanity to corporate health.
Mobilized fears organize aggression against deviants.
Mobilized faith works in love to heal the ills of man.

When healing degenerates into religious argument,
We seek to explain away the healing that offers itself
As itself some new kind of danger come to take us unawares
From our false explanations. We need our devils.
If Jesus casts them out, how can we maintain our demonic drives?
How does one live in a disenthralled world?
In our panic, we even make belief in the devil
A necessary presupposition for belief in God.
We fear if evil would be found unreal, God would be unnecessary.
We must give the product of our fears the appearance
Of substantiality. It is a parasite feeding on our own substance.

The existence of evil is what makes God necessary to exist, we think.
If evil went away, God would go, too, we fear.
God's existence is predicated on our fears.
So we deny to God his own subsistence,
Dependent on no other for his own existence.
We deny God's actual power
To maintain the rule and realm of demons we say we hate.
We need our devils to persuade us we need God to overcome them.
Else we would have to discover another language
To explain our myriad ills and illusions
So highly resistant to every encroaching reality.

Jesus answers our illogic with logic.
A kingdom divided against itself is brought to ruin.
A house divided against itself cannot stand. It falls.
If Satan is schizophrenic, he is divided against himself.
His conflict is self-destructive. How can his kingdom stand?
If you say I cast out devils by Beelzebub,
How does your argument stand up?
By whom do your own sons cast out devils?
Or have you let it slip that it is you, not I,
Who is in league with Satan?
If I cast out devils by the finger of God,
Then the kingdom of God has come upon you.
Satan is opposed not by Satan but by God.
The tyranny of delusion is broken by Reality.

The kingdoms of men,
Those forms of fear constructed socially as reality,
Have reason to fear the reality of God breaking in.
God's kingdom demolishes our myths, chases our devils,
Lays our fears to rest, delivers us to speak anew.


That should finish the argument. It doesn't.
If Jesus' healing be granted, then his authority is questioned.
We cannot accept the facts fully. We do not welcome salvation.
We fear it. To live with Reality is more demanding
Than to live with conventional illusions and shared delusions,
When we give them names of patriotism, law and order,
And doctrines of religion.


Mankind needs more than banishment of devils
And deliverance from superstition to learn to live in reality.
Reality is that difficult realm where our rationale no longer works.
What happens to the house of the soul in men and nations
When the devils are purged? We know by now
That killing people does not do the job. Devils reappear.
We go about our annual housecleanings, our national elections,
Our civic purges, our various resolutions, with glee and gusto.
We seek to rid ourselves of unwholesome influences by mania.
Our puritanic sweep of pornography and other excitements falters.

Our ban takes place behind winking eyes.
The eye of the beholder likes what it sees.
Our prurient interests need pandering to.
Publicized repression is better than sexuality acknowledged.
Our periodic elections pretend to throw the rascals out,
To scour the body politic of corruption we like to live with.
The hypocrisy is that we want to know the grafters to elect them.
Reformers we distrust. Rogues like us in office reassure us.
We do not admit the corruption that is in us—or we do.
We have no intention of really rooting it out.
That would take genuine repentance, a price too high for us.
Exorcism is going further than we ever mean to go.
Now we know why Jesus causes so many people so much trouble.


What happens to all the new regimes of reform, revolution?
They become cruel and stupid and ineffective, unable to replace
Our preference for evil with an internalized good as norm.
The new house is swept clean of former corruptibles hanging on.
The new regime brings in its own menagerie of parasites.
No new affection for the good infects an unrepentant people.
Freedom becomes the greatest of all burdens for contented slaves.
Ten devils return to inhabit what one once held.
All our evils are back, multiplied. We feel at home again.
Do not listen to our complaints. We do not mean them.

After each revolution, reform, and purge,
Devils erupt and materialize out of our own sinful natures
To haunt us and reassure us that the world is as bad as we want it.
New enemies must be conjured up
To keep our world peopled with recognizable devils.
This is how we handle our self-hatred: by projecting it on others.

We keep our devils like a national treasury.
Our kingdoms really depend on making other people devils.
It is as Jesus said. A strong man armed—and nation, too—
Keeps his kingdom, palace, wealth intact by redoubtable defense.
No wonder an affluent society, bent on keeping its goods,
Fears the thieves it makes through plunder, creating enemies.
We make a fetish of national defense to guard what cannot be kept.
We do not notice our precious wealth disappear into hardware.
Spirit drains. The whole people is sucked dry of soul and wealth.
Senseless fear makes us our own worst enemy.
It will not take long before we fail to function.
Defense measures lapse in proliferation.
The law of entropy takes over.
Systems malfunction. Nothing works anymore.
The all-consuming gods of war, devils in disguise of technocracy,
Eat up the national resource and discharge loads overseas.
People's wealth and energies are drained to ward off the future.
All are distressed by a new kind of poverty of abundance.

Then comes the stronger man or nation
To overcome the muscle-bound missilemen.
He takes away our armor of technology in which we put our trust.
The invader comes to divide our spoils when we deplete ourselves,
As once we conquered weaker peoples and stole their land and goods.

That history everyone knows
Who knows the ways of men and nations,
The rise and fall of civilizations.
Not only Indians bit the dust in the plunder of a continent.
We shall bite the dust of history when devils flee and new men come.
A thousand cowboy films blind us to our true history.
We made Indians, gentle folk, into devils, because they were different,
To deny our own devils we projected them into them.

We do not fear the devil as an enemy.
We get along with the devil very well.
The enemy we fear is God who shall come to judge us
And take from us what we took from others.
The kingdom of love and truth and justice is threat to all we have.
We fear our kingdoms of rapaciousness and exploitation
Shall be taken away by men as covetous as we.
There is no armor against God, no way of preventing his coming.
He comes, like the devil, like a thief in the night.
God is the subversive in our midst whose coming

Shatters the false foundation upon which every realm is built.
When God appears in a man, he must be declared subversive,
Because he is. Jesus must be named the devil,
Because we recognize God in him.
It is not really Satan who bothers us.
It is God we fear.

One final way to neutralize Jesus is to praise him.
A woman would exclaim "What a blessed mother to have borne such
    a son!"
For any woman to have such a man as mother or wife
Has occurred to more than one passionate woman.
The organs of feeling are palpable, ardor open and free:
"Blessed is the womb that bore you and the breasts you sucked."
What woman would not want to take Jesus to her breast,
To nurse him, comfort, feed him?
This is, after all, what a woman does. It is very good.
It is her way of relating to life in a man-made world.
It is she who perpetuates the race in a manner fashioned by God.
It is she who brings forth the men who could be, potentially, saviors.

Jesus does not deny the woman's feelings. They are true.
He fully accepts her sexuality unashamedly expressed.
But there is something even more blessed than sexual beatitude.
"Blessed are those who hear the word of God and keep it."

A woman gives up her son when he is born, by degrees till grown.
He becomes an independence outside her.
His need for dependence will change as he grows.
Jesus is the fruit of Mary's womb. He came no other way.
He came that way as God's own Word to man, incarnate, enfleshed.
He was his mother's boy but his Father's Son.
Jesus is God's Word, inseparable from God.
He is Mary's son, inseparable from us.

The word of God cannot be kept from man.
It is not born from us, does not live apart from us.
God's word takes the place of devils in our heart.
It fills the heart with good things, the mind with good ideas.
People with the word of God enfleshed in their hearts
Are the most blessed people in the world,
More blessed, even, than the Mother of our Lord.
They do not possess the saving word to win arguments.
They possess it to prevail and heal.

To be impressed by Jesus is not the proper response
To his mastery over devils.
To possess and use God's saving word
Fills the heart and drives the devils out,
The word of God can even make the dumb to speak.
We know. We do.

# WHENCE SHALL WE BUY BREAD
# IN THE DESERT FOR THESE MEN TO EAT?

**LENT IV**
John 6:1–15

THE problem at first is how to gather a multitude.
The problem of success is satisfying the constituency.
Jesus gathered a following because he healed.
The multitude followed him expecting miracles.
The populace creates the celebrity king.
God alone provides the saviors of mankind.
The crowd creates the situation in which a savior is needed.
It cannot create a savior; it can only recognize him when he comes.
And then it is almost always wrong in its expectations.

Jesus needed distance from the crowds at times,
To think things out, gain perspective, pray.
That's what mountains are for.
From the mountain view he saw the crowd coming,
Inundating the desert to find him.
His mind went to work logistically.
They would all have to eat.
Had anybody thought about that?
The desert is not exactly glutted with supermarkets.

Five loaves and two fish would have to do.
That was all there was.

Jesus multiplied them by inexplicable means.
However done, it started a great festival of sharing.
It sometimes happens that a crowd becomes a community.
Wherever enough food came from, it came.
Everybody recognized the experience for what it was:
A miracle, a wondrous thing, a moment of grace.
It was enough to make them try to crown him king.

Then Jesus did what no politician ever did,
Except some of recent memory.
He left them to go up a mountain by himself
To pray, or write poetry, or do some other lofty thing.
The crowd was disappointed and perplexed.
What more did he want from them than their allegiance?
What more did they want from him than bread?
They wanted to capture a moment of grace,
Politicize it, perpetuate it, systematize it, institutionalize it,
Rather than accept its uniqueness as a transforming experience.
What makes a desert, that food be scarce?
What makes a crowd go out looking for a mass experience?
What makes people place such a high burden on leadership
For the fulfillment of their material wants?
Who is fool enough to promise what he can't deliver?

Our deserts are man-made.
Once fertile valleys were deforested.

The land was exploited till it dried out and bleached sand.
Water burrowed underground in subterranean rivers
To escape the surface plunder and disregard.
There was always land enough for grain and grain for bread.
Men sought their own without regard to ecological balance,
Plundering man and land, leaving deserts as their legacy.
The sins of the fathers are visited upon their children.
Pollution is our bequest to our children,
Poisoning land and sky and water for generations to come,
Mortgaging the future for our momentary satisfactions.
What miracles can a new king do to deliver us from that?
What can kings do against stupidity and unrepented sin?

We feed the hungry mouths of combustible engines
And huff and puff all over the land we turn to desert.
While actual children of actual people
Grow gaunt and swollen with actual hunger,
Because there is not enough money to buy them bread
In our deserts which exclude the poor from life and livelihood.

Not enough money? Of course there is enough money.
But our money is for making deserts, not for feeding hungry people.
Congressional committees plead helplessness to relieve the poor.
We denourish our foods, adding additives,
Serving up our calories by non-nutritional food
To our own privileged children to make sure starvation spreads.

Money and not food multiplies to widen the desert of our greed.
So we seek kings to provide us miracle, mystery, husks of bread.

Into this desert of our own making
Come music makers and prophets and love-children
Wearing long hair, beards and beads. Gentle folk,
They preach and practice a gospel of sharing,
Hallucinating private visions of the social good.
The community of sharing is experienced and everybody finds it
   groovy.
Woodstock becomes a momentary city of grace in a rural pasture.

Woodstock was a miracle, as few would deny.
Altamount was a disaster, as everybody finally had to admit.
It is a large step from an experience of grace and joy to a New Nation.
A new nation like that requires a new kind of people.
It needs a whole lifetime of giving, sharing, multiplying resources.
No king can do that for us. We must do it ourselves.
We must become a people prepared for the coming of King Jesus.
We must multiply bread and fish and food for all
And see that nobody gets left out when the basket's passed.
"Ho, every one who thirsts, come to the waters;
And he who has no money, come, buy and eat!
Come, buy wine and milk without money and without price.
Why do you spend money for that which is not bread,
And your labor for that which does not satisfy?" (Isaiah 55:1–2).

# JUDICA ME, DEUS

*Introit:*
>    JUDGE me, O God, and plead my cause against an ungodly
>       nation.
O deliver me from the deceitful and unjust man,
For thou art the God of my strength.

*Psalm:*
O Send out thy light and thy truth; let them lead me;
Let them bring me unto thy holy hill.

*Coda:*
"The trial proved the system works."
So saith the prosecutor about assorted "revolutionaries"
Disported before old grads as "freaking fags."
The system works. Ungodly nations have their way.
Seven defendants, for contempt of court, lay shorn
In Cook County Jail, society's contemptibles,
Poor and black, maunder there forgotten and alone,
Without bail. "Evil men" all—else why there?
From Galilee to Jerusalem he crossed state lines
To incite a riot. A "festival of life" he called it.
He did not pass by Pilate's system of surveillance

Unnoticed. Legionnaires, armed for battle, wait
In riot formation for festivities to begin. "Blessed
Is he who comes in the name of the Lord," Yippies yell.
Bar-Abbas ("Son of the Father"), jailed from last time,
Hopes they will get him out. He will get out, when Jesus comes
To take his place. The system works, revolving ebb
And flow of prisoners, as each new fool tests
Himself against intransigence. There were twelve
Who breathed together in conspiracy. Informers know
Their names, can point them out, will testify in court.
Just one undercover agent will do to betray within,
The *agent provocateur*. False witnesses will do the rest.
Officials have decided in advance of arrest. "It is
Expedient that one man die for all," says Caiaphas.
And all his clergy say "Amen." Sanhedrins and
Executive boards concur. The church is pledged.
The system works. That's what's at stake. Court
Convenes in early morning for speedy trial. Demonstrators
May not show up on time. Administration rabble rousers
Work crowds of public watchers on to passion pitch.
Not-so-silent majorities outshout Freedom's holy few
With long-savored seasoned obscenities, like "Crucify!"
The judge regards assent that justice rules,
When only men must die. Procurators have their clout,
No doubt of it. Witnesses are procured to tell their lies.

"We heard him say he would destroy the temple."
He does not deny the charge. His silence means consent.
"What further need have we of witnesses?" say politicians
In churchly robes, waxing publicly indignant for the record.
He goes to die the scheduled death upon the cross.
And then the public panic starts. "Guard the temple,
Seal the tomb, secure the city, lest angry mobs explode
And patriots infiltrate to body snatch." Conspiracies
Abound in paranoid minds. How like criminals officials think!
Those who stir a people's passions for freedom find
A dispassionate court to cool their own. Contempt
Of court is silenced, professionally, by marshals trained
To lock jaws. A facial blow restores respect. A crown
Of thorns will do for ridicule, or purple robes, or shaved
Beards and heads. Let his passion now begin. Lead him to
His holy hill of execution. His death shall prove
Our system works. GLORY BE, etc.

— Chicago, Judica Sunday, Spring 1970
The Trial of the Chicago Seven (Eight) [Ten] took place all during Lent
to its judgment near Judica Sunday. The basic charges were denied by the
jury. Other judgments were appealed to higher courts. The basic punish-
ment meted out to defendants and defense lawyers was stiff prison sen-
tences for "contempt of court." "The trial proved our system works." It
did what it was designed to do: suppress dissent by punishing peace-
makers as examples to discourage civil protest against a criminal war.

# KINGS, GO FORTH!

**PALM SUNDAY**
Matthew 21:1–9

A KING who would rule unstable people must hold the guns.
Power is what makes kings in our world. If Jesus
Is to be a king in our world, he will need more
Than crowds shouting hosannas. He will need to demonstrate
The power that goes with rule and be recognized
By all his willing subjects as legitimate.
Jesus is just as mortal as any aspirant to throne
Or incumbent king. Power does not yield; it must be taken.
To seize the throne in bloodless coup d'etat risks blood.
People may hail Jesus King in Caesar's hearing.
Displacing Caesar is another thing from riding
Into a captive city on a donkey before cheering crowds
Which name one king before the fact. That political gesture
Is a good way to get oneself killed. On any Friday,
Executioners can nail usurpers to the cross.

Let him rule from there over his whole pitiful kingdom.
Let him be king of the powerless.
Let outcasts claim their outlaw as their king.
He poses no threat to Rome or any stable throne.
The world he rules is one of fantasy, no real one.
He said himself his kingdom was not of this world.
So why would serious kings worry about him as threat to them?
Jesus will build no empire from the throne of the cross.
Who would follow him? Would you? Would I? Would we?

We need a new definition of royalty if Jesus would be king.
We need one anyhow, since he is.
What is this realm which lies inside minds
And is not subject to authority of church or state
But chooses Christ for King?

We need a new definition of royalty,
Because a new king is enthroned in hearts everywhere,
Defying national boundaries, claiming earth itself as realm.
Jesus Christ is Prophet, Priest, and King.
He has made us willing subjects, kings and priests before God.
We are sent to all temporary ruling establishments.
Kings, go forth! Do your thing!
Go humbly and in peace. It is his way. Get used to it.
"Blessed is he who comes in the name of the Lord. Hosanna!"

# COMMUNION

**MAUNDY THURSDAY**

HE took the bread, embodied it;
He shared the wine and blooded it.
Uncomprehendingly,
They ate and drank of it.

# PILATE

WELL, what would you have done?
Have you ever faced a mob?
Have you ever tried to maintain order
In this damned disorderly world?
Have you never sacrificed a principle
Or a person to maintain peace?
Do you think it easy
To rule a province or a country?
Try it some time.
Try to please all the people.
Try to do what is right.
You'll soon lose your ideals.

You speak glibly of justice,
Condemn official ineptitude,
Extol abstract principles,
Decry moral turpitude—
You who have to be dragged
Off to the polls to vote.
You would not know an HR bill
If you saw one.
You bask in your smug insolence
And *talk* politics.

**48**

*You* would never run
For public office.
When did you ever even
Write your congressman?

Don't talk to me
About the sins of officialdom.
When the showdown comes,
*You'll* never back me up.
You'll hide in the shadows,
Lurk in the crowd.
When it's all over,
You'll yell bloody murder.
I know your kind!

When you'll stand up for what you believe in,
When you'll defend the defenseless
And open your mouth for the poor and needy—
Your own Bible tells you that!—
When you'll risk your skin
For the truth you proclaim so loudly,
Then I'll listen.
When private morals match public expectation
Perhaps "justice" will not have a hollow ring.
I want to hear truth in the market place,
Not just from pulpits and college lecture halls.

You have your own little world of tyranny.
You're not so just! Ask your own children—
Or employees—if they dare answer.
What do you care about the truth?
Would you care to have your decisions reviewed?
How would you stand up under the glare of publicity?

I'll take Jesus before you any day.
Now, there's a man!
He never flinched.
He said he was a king from another world.
If so, he's a better king
Than we'll ever find in this one.
He bore his cross
Like every man rolled into one.
God, I wish
I could live and die like that.

They say he will come back,
That he'll be judge of every man
Who lives and dies.
I hope he does.
I'll get a better brand
Of justice from him
Than he got from me,
Or I'll ever get from you.

# PIETA

NOW hangs the head,
Chin resting on sunken chest,
Beard strands covering ashen flesh,
Heart no longer pumping blood
Through open wounds.

Now hangs the dead,
Sagging unfeelingly,
Limbs held by stubborn nails.
They will draw them out
To take him down.

Hammer, hammer, striking hard,
You've done your work,
Your aim was true:
You aimed at hands and feet,
And caught his heart.

Laugh now,
You howling human jackals.
Show yellowed teeth and bloody fang,
You carnivorous bipeds

**GOOD FRIDAY**

Who strip flesh from body
To see if he has a soul,
To see what makes the Son of God
Tick inside.

Weep now,
You who love him,
Your only hope.
He alone stands between
You and the grave.

Take him down gently.
Let artists note your *pieta.*
Wrap him in swaddling clothes
For Death's long night—
But not too tightly.
He will not need them long.

# FREE AMONG THE DEAD

IT is a vast unchallenged land.
   Its frontiers are unguarded.
No one comes to attack.
From its bourne no traveller escapes.

It numbers numberless
Numbed and captive souls.
Its entrance is just
A hole in the ground
Six feet wide
And six feet deep.

It catches time in a net
And immobilizes life.
Its space is measured
In spiritual dimensions.
Its time spans eternity.
There are no clocks
Or setting suns
Or familiar stars.

It is the realm of darkness
And silence, where whispers cannonade
Along the corridors of eternity.
It is a place of black fire
Which sears but does not smoke,
Consuming tortured souls.

It claims even living men
Above the ground, dispirited,
Dead to God and others,
Dead in conscience,
Dead to feeling,
Dead in life,
Habituated,
Compulsive,
Automated.

In that shadowed land
A light shone forth.
Christ came to conquer death,
To beard the devil in his lair,
Free among the dead.

He rose to lead humanity
Out of all the graves
To bright, white light and life.

EASTER

# CROSSWINDS

CROSSWINDS blow at Easter,
   Blowing north and blowing south,
Sowing warmth and chilling doubt,
Blowing east and blowing west,
Rising sun dispelling rest,
Rousing life among the blest.

Crosswinds blow at Easter.
From the north the last chill
Finger of cold upon the dead,
Freezes faith in crocus hearts,
Which bloom too soon before
The sun's full warmth is here
To stay. The chill of doubt
Crystallizes dew of hope,
And rocks roll back in place
To seal the chambers of the dead
Against a debatable resurrection.
The chill wind says,
"The sun warms not.
It's much too far for rays to penetrate
And quicken flesh or liven bones.
My ice shall cover all and immobilize
The green leaf of hope.
There is no life or resurrection,

Only the long winter's night without end
Under perpetual doubt's polar icecap.
If you doubt doubt, feel my chill wind
And believe in death's despair."

Crosswinds blow at Easter.
From the south the first warm
Breath of life tingles blood,
Scents the nostrils, quickens pulse,
Buds the trees and opens earth
With a billion resurrections
Of only sleeping plants.
Life conquers death
When the south wind blows.
The south wind of the Gospel
Brings good news that Christ is risen,
Revivifying wearied spirits,
Embodying resurrection hope.

Crosswinds blow at Easter.
From the west come tornadoes
Of human conflict, clashing ideologies,
Ravaging earth with explosive hailstones
And mixing clouds of radioactive dust
With streams of power propaganda.
Various "isms" fan the masses

High and low into instability.
Destruction wastes at noonday
In the darkened history of man.
Westerly winds of technology
Gone mad, dehumanize man,
Despirit the universe in the name
Of secular totalitarianisms,
Based on the holy writ of science
And dialectics of materialism.
These do not chill but sear
The soul of man, rendering him
Automaton. The sepulchre stone,
A concrete slab, shuts humanity in
From outside light and hope.

Crosswinds blow at Easter.
From the Orient come gentle
Easterlies—mystic breezes
From an ancient world, mysterious
In detachment, against the
Planet's spin, as if from other
Worlds. Their pantheism stirs
"Beat" generations of Occident
Into intimations of beatific
Visions which lie beyond

The facade of crude hard facts,
Clothes of materiality. The easterlies
Do not herald resurrection,
But sense of spirit
Beyond psychologies and myth:
Universes populated with flaming suns,
Ghosts that walk in animals
And hide in trees. Stone
Dissolves to sand and spirits
Join the breeze that talks.

Crosswinds blow at Easter.
Nature stirs, love is roused,
Persons flower, hope revives.
Those in Christ are no longer children,
Tossed about by every wind of doctrine,
But built upon the rock
Of him who moved the rock
Of Death's sepulchre at Easter.

Another wind blows at Easter.
It comes not from around the globe,
From north or south or east or west.
It comes from above. *Creator Spiritus*
Brooded once over chaos
From which our earth was formed.

God's Holy Breath broods now
Over chaotic humanity to give new life in Christ,
To shape a new humanity,
Into the Body of our risen Lord.

Do not be blown about
By every wind of doctrine.
Become inspired by Holy Spirit,
Sent from God through Christ for man.
Receive new life, new spirit, hope.
Experience resurrection in baptismal grace.
Rise to new life in Christ, here and now,
In your own life, from your own past,
For your own new future
Of human being come alive.
God's word stirs dead souls to kindle life
And Spirit brews the elixir of love
For all the chalices of human flesh.
The sacraments are moving in the universe.
The Spirit of life and power
Who raised the Shepherd of the sheep
From the dead dark place where no winds blow
Will in our own time raise us
And all who hear the Spirit's call
To eternal life with Christ in God.
The Spirit is blowing in the wind.

# NEW LIFE AMONG THE CRUCIFIED

**EASTER I**
John 20:19–31

THE crosses stand empty now,
   Silhouetted against the sky.
They will be used again
By an economy-minded administration.
No use to throw good wood away.
Crosses are designed for utility.
They are made to last.

Who knows the names of those
Who carried crosses on their backs
Before their crosses carried them?
Strange irony of turnabout!

Their loads have long since been
   Delivered,
      Dispatched,

            Disposed,
                Interred.

They lie among the unremembered dead,
    Unmourned,
        Not missed,
Recorded in some obscure clerk's registry.

There are many ways to crucify a man.
The cross is only one.
Death utilizes countless strategies.
They all come out the same.
All roads lead to a common grave.

Hope flickers wistfully
But withers in the face of reality.
They all succumb at last.
Jesus Christ and Anne Frank:
Innocence incinerated in hatred.
Whatever hope there is
Must be discovered in the breathless world.

Things would be different
If one stirred to life again,
Resurrected, victorious, immortalized,
And walked among the crucified
To give them a founded hope.

New life among the crucified
Should wear flesh and blood.

Our Lord Jesus Christ wore just that.
He alone among the countless dead revived,
Shook off his winding sheet,
Left his "last resting place"
Scarcely used.

He showed himself alive
Among the ancient crucified
In the Stygian darkness of the dead.
How many before Thomas reached forth
To handle risen flesh and finger recent wounds?

New life appeared for gently crucified.
A woman crucified by grief,
Nails invisible piercing aching heart,
Mary Magdalene wept beside the empty tomb.

Jesus called her name, spoke to her.
Her sorrow turned to joy and melancholy fled.
New life appeared among the crucified.

Ten men crucified by fear
Hid behind barricaded doors
To shut fear out, in vain.
Their fears came in with them.
Our Lord appeared and all fears vanished.
Knowing dispels the fear of unknown consequences.
New life appeared among the crucified.

One man was crucified by doubt,
Torn between the wish to believe
And the harsh realities of universal experience.
Dead men do not come back to life. Never!
Only pragmatic proof could warrant Resurrection faith
As no mere wish.

Does risen life submit to such a test?
Is it not beyond experiment?
Does not its Presence suffice to kindle hope and faith?
Must it be seen, touched, felt?
What do flesh and blood prove, after all,
Except the wearer is alive.

Unbound life is worn within.
Christ bids Thomas see and feel
To shame his faith and banish doubt.
New life appeared among the crucified.

Another man was crucified by guilt.
He had persecuted risen Christ himself,
Inflicted wounds upon his living body, church.
Christ invited Paul to crucify himself
And come to life anew.
"I have been crucified with Christ," he said.
"It is no longer I who lives.
It is Christ who lives within me.
The life I live now in the flesh
I live by faith in God's own Son,
Who loved and gave himself for me."
New life appeared among the crucified.

The world's crucified today
Raise helpless eyes for possible deliverance.
Sufferers wracked with pain,
Prisoners in political hells,
Incurables held in tightening grip of terminal diseases,
Scapegoats nailed by others' hate,
Families torn with dissension,

Walking wounded with ulcerated love,
Young and old burned with the acids of modernity,
Ghetto-dwellers pinned in squalor of poverty,
Losers outclassed in a stratified society,
Individualists marked for death by mass conformity,
Believers holding fast an embattled Christian faith,
Seekers groping their way to God's light,
Martyrs harrassed by religious persecution,
Captive peoples oppressed by freedom's blackout,
Parishioners lulled in churches dedicated to success,
Confessors everywhere who suffer for the name of Christ.
New life appears among the crucified today.

Christ is risen! Let the cross come!
It is our sign of freedom and life.
New life appears *only* among the crucified.

# SHEEPMEN AND MEN-SHEEP

IN the Bible they were shepherds.
  Our Old West called them "Sheep-men."
Shepherds carried staffs and slings.
Sheepmen carried rifles and knives.
Shepherds fought wolves and mountain lions.
Sheepmen did, too; in addition, cattlemen.
Both looked for wolves in sheep's clothing.
Some of both were bad and good.
Sheep and wolves knew the difference,
Sometimes.

Now take the Good Shepherd.
His sheep know his voice,
Recognize and follow him,
Confidently.
He does not turn and run,
But gives his life to save the sheep.
Jesus' staff is a cross.

Pastors are his undershepherds.
Unarmed sheepmen, gathering human
Flocks, seeking strays, calling
Out aloud invitations and warnings,

**EASTER II**
John 10:11–16

Healing wounded, torn souls.
Not unused to criticism
(Human sheep talk back).

Are not the people sheep?
A nation of sheep plays follow the leader
In automobiles and politics.
They wear alpaca coats
And drink martinis dry.
Human sheep operate computers and guide
Celestial missiles to scan the universe,
Themselves unguided by any word from God.
Sheep who fly by radar and live by instinct
Cultivate the intellect and boast of reason's supremacy.
Dominated by apathetic passions and undifferentiated emotion,
They are irrational rationalists in an age some call "absurd."

Human sheep sneer at salvation
Now that they have learned to live
Technologically,
Imagining that life is only a matter of technique.
Poor lost sheep!
They do not even know they are lost!
Poor fleeced sheep,
Shorn naked by electric power shears
That glint so prettily in the sun,

Products of the age of stainless steel.
Poor mesmerized sheep,
Fascinated by mechanical reproductive images
On television, magazines, and technicolored screens,
Lulled by the smooth sales pitch,
The soft sell of grey-flanneled fleecers
Out to wrap them up in a "big ball of wax."

No wonder they are so bewildered
When an economic recession bogs them down,
When suddenly they find themselves standing
On the brink of atomic holocaust,
When their pastures greened with dollar bills
Brown and blow away with inflation's winds.
Black sheep offend them,
But wolves still pull wool over their eyes.
Older sheep need bifocals plus
Social security to see them through.
Gossip columnists duly publicize
The private escapades of wandering sheep.
The Good Shepherd is still the only One
Who goes in to find, salve, bandage, heal,
Not to exploit but to redeem,
Though now he makes his rounds
In a helicopter or a compact car.

# A LITTLE WHILE

S EE you in a little while,"
Says Jesus in valedictory after Easter.

**EASTER III**
John 16:16–21

That's too soon for some folks.
Only Christians want him back.

Nothing makes people happier
Than to see those dead whom they hate.
Think how the world rejoiced when Hitler died.
We just cannot stand the sight of some people.
"Undesirables" don't have to do anything at all.
They just have to look different, dress different, talk different.
It is enough to want them out of sight, out of town, out of mind.
If they won't go peacefully we have devised methods of eviction.
We've run them out of town on rails, tarred and feathered.
We've put them in jails, the toilets of our courts,
And flushed them down the drain, a one-way ticket to oblivion.
We hang them, electrocute them, gas them, crucify them.
That's where Jesus can go, and good riddance.
And he can take all his sleazy friends along.
Jesus can go to hell, so far as the world's concerned.
He knows it. Disciples know it. Church people don't know it.
Americans don't know what we are doing
Any more than Jews did who killed prophets,
Or Romans did who crucified barbarians,
Or Germans did who cremated Jews,

Or Americans did who massacred the Indians and the Vietnamese.
We always think "The Final Solution to the Human Problem"
Is to kill those we do not like, who are in our way,
Whom we blame for all our troubles.

What makes the world happy
Makes sad those of us who love Jesus.
How could anyone want to kill him,
Whose heart, we know, is full of love for all?
But then, why would anyone want to kill
Mohandas Gandhi or Martin Luther King
Or college students at Kent and Jackson State?
How could such things make people glad?
But glad they were, Americans in majority.
"They should have shot them all," was said
When only four were killed at Kent.

"See you in a little while," says Jesus.
"Now you have sorrow.
Not only will you miss me.
They shall put you out of the churches.
The time will come when whoever kills you
Will think he is doing God a service.
They will do these things to you
Because they have not known the Father or me."

Incredible!
But it happens all the time.

It is the pain of childbirth.
The new humanity that is being born into the world
Does not come without travail.
To focus on the pain forgets the birth
And fears only the death of hope.
It only takes a little while,
Until the pain ceases.
It is forgotten in the face of a new joy.
A child is born into the world.

"I will see you again,
In a little while,
And your heart will rejoice.
No man will be able
To take that joy from you."

It is not the day of jubilation yet,
For this promise still waits to be kept.
But we had better start counting
The intervals between contractions.
They are getting shorter.
It will only take a little while longer.

# THE SPIRIT OF TRUTH

**EASTER IV**
John 16:5–15

WHY should Jesus leave the scene
When Easter's just begun
And the Resurrection of human life
Has just commenced?
How can his Movement continue
With its leader gone?

Jesus leaves, he says,
Because it is expedient
(A most unusual word for him)
For us that he should go.
When he leaves
He will send his Holy Spirit
To fill his followers.
The Spirit of Truth
Will lead us into all truth.

Christ multiplies himself in us.
His Spirit of Truth fills us all.
He makes the many one,
Transforms the one into countless many.
Believers coalesce and move out

To converge upon an unwary world.
His Spirit fortifies our own.
He comforts us in persecution and distress.
He prevails in weakness to overthrow the strong.
He does it bloodlessly, by word and act and insinuation.


The Spirit of Truth
Makes its own way among men.
No ruler can stay its coming,
Control its course,
Inhibit its strength,
Or prevent its victory.


The victory of truth in one man
Is a threat to false establishments everywhere.
"Where the Spirit of the Lord is,
There is also liberty."
"The free man is lord of all,
Subject to none" (Martin Luther).
The Spirit is the greatest threat
To those who would control others
In the name of God and man.
The Spirit thrives in weakness,

Its germinating place,
Developing its own power.
Free men can become servants.
When they do, watch out.
God stoops to human flesh to serve man
And raises it to glory with him.
God makes his power perfect in weakness,
In the seething masses beneath all thrones,
In the hot core of earth which moves the crust,
When the Spirit moves the mass, thrones totter, tumble.
The earth quakes along every line of human fault.

Knowledge is not power.
It only serves power as its captive.
Truth is the ultimate, unfettered power.
Truth is the secret which unlocks the universe.
Truth unlocks us, makes us vulnerable,
Liberates us to serve God and man in love and truth.
Those whose power lives off devouring weaker others
Rise to Truth's hook baited with weakness
And are caught by Spirit.
In men of truth the Spirit ranges free.
In men of power Truth sticks
In the eyes, ears, nose, and throat,
Which all the wild lashing about cannot dislodge.

Easter is God's Liberation Movement for mankind.
The pioneer of our salvation led the way
Through cross and pain to victory over fear and death.
When his Spirit comes at Pentecost,
God breaks out everywhere into human experience.
Men of truth speak out boldly,
Not counting the cost.
Freedom's fire spreads.
Judgment Day has begun in the world,
When men of power
Who seek to kill spirit and God in man
Find their power fails,
That Truth prevails.
God uncoils to strike their power
From forms of human weakness,
Infiltrating, undermining, jamming
All systems of oppression of human spirit.

Truth and power, when they meet
Recognize each other as enemies instinctively.

It is not good news to Caiaphas
Or Pilate that Christ returns.
It is not good news to dictators
That truth cannot be crushed.

It is not good news to controllers
That the uncontrollable has announced itself.
It is not good news to the world
That it is judged.

It is good news
To those who sit in darkness,
Who begin to see the great light.
Truth has worn through
The false facade
Of all its counterfeits.
It is about to emerge again,
Unbidden, hitherto unexpressed,
From its dormant hiding place.
It will make its way in the world.
It cannot be stopped.
God is on the move among his people.
The Spirit of Truth
Leads the way
Into all truth.

FROM the Van Allen radiation belts,
  From streams of charged particles,
Plasmas in the solar wind of space,
From undetected effects of cosmic rays,
And from fallout of Strontium 90:
  GOOD LORD, DELIVER US!

From high levels of unemployment,
From low levels of employment of the employed,
From mere mathematics of management:
  GOOD LORD, DELIVER US!

From personal prejudices of professors,
From anti-intellectualism of preachers,
From false superiority of inferior students,
From the jargon of meaningless words,
And from compulsory miseducation:
  GOOD LORD, DELIVER US!

From reckless drivers of high-powered automobiles,
From ritual chants of television commercials,
From nihilism and forced depression in our movies,
From explanations of our abstract art,
And from domination by changing status symbols:
  GOOD LORD, DELIVER US!

# LITANY FOR THE AGE OF SPACE, STEEL, AND ATOM

**EASTER V**
John 16:23–30

From enemies of social change,
From mass builders of new slums,
From indifferent public agencies,
From yellow journalism and political propaganda,
From fanatics of extremes on left and right,
From majority rule without minority rights,
And from dehumanization in technocratic societies:
    GOOD LORD, DELIVER US!

From price fixers and sellers of inferior goods,
From overcrowding on inadequate public transportation,
From the dirt and soot and smog of the city,
And from endless triplicate forms:
    GOOD LORD, DELIVER US!

From churches dedicated to statistical success,
Forgetful of ministries of redemption and reconciliation,
From profiteers of prophecy,
And from the deadness with which we infuse our liturgies:
    GOOD LORD, DELIVER US!

For all who labor in thy world to manifest thy love,
To sow thy seed and spread thy word,
To proclaim thy Gospel and reclaim lost souls,
Who gather thy people for prayer and praise,
And hold forth the honor of thy Name:
    WE BESEECH THEE TO HEAR US, GOOD LORD!

# ASCENSION

# ANABASIS: ASCENSION

UP! That's the way to go!
    Up, out, and away! The transcendent
Beckons us out of our place, out of our time,
Out of our skins, out of our imaginations.
We clawed our way out of the mud of prehistory
To command the plains and ride the seas,
Surface men come into our own.
We are restless on the mere waves of history,
Fretful on the plains with mere plows
To furrow earth and make it obedient
To imperial commands: "Grow! Yield! Produce!"
Intermittently we seek diversionary excitement
In wars over territories we know not how to live in
In peace. Between times we build great cities,
Spilling houses over landscapes.
We take special pride in towers, spires,
Skyscrapers. They point up, out, and away.
Our eyes have always looked up unto the hills,

Mountains, the tall trees. Skyscrapers don't
Wave in the air or leaf in summer. Pentagons and
Merchandise marts just sit there in dull regularity,
Pretending they are mountains. Earthbound, they do not
Lead the eye upward and outward. They compress
And repress, enclose and foreclose, and block the view.
The sky covers all, moves and blues and blackens,
Reddens, clouds, and clears, unrestricted,
Tantalizing man to voyage further. Man responds.
The rocket sits on the launching pad. Men sit in it,
Waiting out the countdown to zero. Then it's up,
Out, and away—to the moon, around the earth,
Searching space. There is no longer "up,"
We say sophisticatedly. There is only "out"
And "away." So why do we stand looking into
Empty space where they went? They'll be back.
And someday we'll be "there."

# THE WAY, THE TRUTH, AND THE LIFE

**SUNDAY AFTER ASCENSION**
John 15:26–16:4

CHRIST is the Way, the Truth, the Life.

He is the Way that leads past Calvary,
  Down Death's steep decline,
    Out through Resurrection Rock,
      Up the mount of Ascension,
        Into the blue eternity of Life
          For all who call God "Father."

He is the Truth, if men will believe it,
  Seek it, know it, hold it;
    If men will have him,
      Ridiculed, hated, spurned,
        Dismissed with faint praise,
          Locked up in tawdry pictures,
            Excluded from real life,
              His truth too true to bear.

He is the Life, if men will live beyond
   Passion's present urgings,
      Today's acquisitiveness,
         Yesterday's unfinished history,
            Tomorrow's hazardous blueprints,
               Yesterday's sorrows, tomorrow's fears, today's despair.

He is the Way to God that few walk.
He is the Truth which never dies, though often crucified.
He is the Life of God in man availably personified.
He is the Way which wends through time to eternity.
He is the Truth which shines in darkness in every age.
He is the Life whose continuity is unbroken eternally.

A Cross was reared
   To thwart the Way,
      To contradict the Truth,
         To cut the line of Life.

The Cross posted the sign of his Way:
   "Dead End" on Calvary.
Above his head, in superscription, Truth
   Was nailed to the cross with him
      To show its pragmatic uselessness.

They cut the line of Life at three o'clock.
"Three o'clock and all's well! God is dead!"

The Way is successfully barricaded.
No one will go that way through life.
The Truth is snuffed out.
It will bother you no more.
The life which animated him
Has been exhaled into the afternoon breeze.

"What shall we do with the body?"

"Bury it, of course!"
Now, and twenty centuries later
It keeps coming stubbornly to life again.
That is no way for a corpse to act.
Do not the Christians know Christianity is passé?

From now on roads will be marked sensibly on maps.
They will not be spiritual vapor trails in cosmology.
They will not trace the wandering footsteps of an itinerant Jew,
His passing awaited eagerly by roadside lepers,
Blind beggars, raving maniacs, poor widows, dead sons.
Now traffic may move freely and swiftly again,
Down newly constructed freeways to faraway places,

Past walled-in institutions which hide men's misery,
Through invisible ghettoes of the impacted poor.
The crooked has been made straight with engineered curves.
We can travel at sixty-five miles per hour, or more.
*Via Dolorosa,* indeed!
*Via mundi* is straighter, more direct.

From now on Truth will be limited to classroom discussions.
"Expediency, relativity, tradition,
Mores, customs, myths" are more workable terms
With which to meet life as we know it.

Modern plumbing has solved the problem of the Samaritan woman.
Running water, hot and cold, is piped to her kitchen faucet.
She need never thirst again.
No longer will women spend time at a village well
Drawing water, engaging in discussions with strange men
About metaphysical problems.

Never again will Pilate have his deliberations
Disturbed by questions which belong to philosophy and religion,
Not to politics.

From now on Life will be confined to temporary quarters,
Measured out in computed doses.

Watches will tick off the seconds of its duration.
Calendars will define it.
Schedules will regulate it.
Doctors will take its pulse.
Hospitals will seek to prolong it.
Never again shall eternity commandeer the present.

All this was accomplished by the Cross.

But God had different plans.
He opened up the Way blocked by the Cross,
Breaking open the tomb, rolling away the rock.
He vindicated Truth
Making it judge of everything,
Its validation, Resurrection.
He gave Good News to preach universally:
The liberation of all human life from every form of death.
He healed the wound of death,
The cut lifeline of eternity.
He gives eternal life to all who seek it
In Jesus Christ.
His Life is now our own.

Stop that man Paul!

He has torn the Cross from the ground.
He has removed the barrier on the Way.
He is carrying it before him like a guidon.
He is leading thousands over Calvary after Jesus.
He has carried it all over the empire.
Our empires cannot survive if Christ prevails.


Stop those men Peter and John!
They will not stop talking about Jesus.
They are civilly disobedient, ignoring our injunctions.
They offend against law and order and stir the multitude.
We shall teach them to fear men rather than God.


Kill those Christians in the arena!
Somebody make them stop singing those hymns.
Where is their sense of propriety?
Don't they know where they are?
Don't they know what is happening to them?
Don't they know they are criminals in prison?
Don't they know they are being executed for crimes against the state?
They act as if they are free.
They keep wanting eternal life.
We will kill them if they do not stop it.

A thousand crosses go up again
    To block the Way,
        To crucify the Truth,
            To kill the life of Christ in men.
                To no avail.

"The blood of the martyrs
Is the seed of the church,"
Said Tertullian.

"You shall be my witnesses,"
Said Christ to friends.
"You shall be my martyrs."
And then he left.

Who will be his witness
When he's gone?
When his friends are dead?
How can a "gone" Jesus
Inspire new followers
To go his Way?

Shall we list the names?
Consult the dictionary of saints.
You have heard of Martin Luther

And of Martin Luther King,
Of Dietrich Bonhoeffer
And Father Delp.
Consult your newspapers.
They will tell you
Of priests named Berrigan
Nuns, and others.

Most names
Are not known.
They are written
In the Book of Life.
Where is yours written?
Which Way do you walk?